SMART ABOUT...

CHOCOLATE

A Sweet History

By Garrett Myers

By Sandra Markle

Illustrated by Charise Mericle Harper

Cover illustrated by Maryann Cocca-Leffler

Grosset & Dunlap • New York

For my husband, Skip Jeffery, whose love is the
only thing better than chocolate—S.M.

Acknowledgement:
The author would like to thank the following people for
sharing their enthusiasm and expertise: Dr. Mark Guiltinan, Director, the Cacao
Molecular Biology Program at Pennsylvania State University and Judy Hogarth,
Public Affairs, Hershey Foods Corporation.

p. 5: © Michael Lent; p. 7: © Hershey Community Archives; p. 8: © Hershey Community Archives;
p. 21: © Hershey Community Archives; p. 22, top: © Hershey Community Archives; p. 22, bottom:
courtesy of Hershey Entertainment & Resorts; p. 23: © Andre Jenny/Focus Group/Picture Quest; p. 24:
© AP-World Wide Photo; p. 25, top: © Hershey Community Archives; p. 25, bottom: © Rosanne Guararra

Library of Congress Cataloging-in-Publication Data

Markle, Sandra.
   Chocolate : a sweet history / by Sandra Markle ; illustrated by Charise Mericle Harper.
      p. cm. — (Smart about history)
Includes bibliographical references.
   ISBN 0-448-43480-6 (pbk.) — ISBN 0-448-43566-7 (hardcover) 1. Cookery (Chocolate)—Juvenile literature.
2. Chocolate—History—Juvenile literature. [1. Chocolate—History.] I. Harper, Charise Mericle, ill. II. Title.
III. Series.
   TX767.C5M27 2004
   641.6'374—dc22   2003024570

ISBN 0-448-43480-6 (pbk)   10 9 8 7 6 5 4 3 2 1
ISBN 0-448-43566-7 (GB)   10 9 8 7 6 5 4 3 2 1

From the desk of
Ms. Brandt

Dear Class,
  We have been learning about so many exciting events from the past. Now you may choose a subject that is of special interest to you for your report.
  You may write about something that happened thousands of years ago or about something that happened not so very long ago - maybe when your parents or your grandparents were your age. It's up to you!

  Here are some questions you might want to think about:

🍎 What made you pick your topic?

🍎 Did you learn anything that really surprised you?

  Good luck and have fun!

                              Ms. Brandt

Chock-full of Chocolate

DAD SAYS EVEN HIS GRANDMOTHER LIKED CHOCOLATE.

CHOCOLATE IS DELICIOUS!

We ♥ Chocolate!

I love chocolate. My whole family does. On our last vacation, we went to Hershey's Chocolate World in Pennsylvania. It was the best trip ever. There's an amusement park and you can also learn a lot about chocolate. So it was easy for me to pick a subject for my report. Also, I figured if I did an experiment with chocolate, I could eat the results. (And I did!)

PENNSYLVANIA

HERSHEY

NEW YORK CITY

PITTSBURGH

HARRISBURG

PHILADELPHIA

WILMINGTON

POWDERED CHOCOLATE + WATER = CHOCOLATE DRINK

Until a couple of hundred years ago, people did not eat chocolate. They drank it. And I'm not talking about hot chocolate. It was just powdered chocolate mixed with water. The really weird thing is that the chocolate tasted bitter, because it didn't have any sugar in it. I'm pretty sure I wouldn't have liked it. Back then, chocolate was so valuable, only rich people could afford it. So maybe I wouldn't have even had the chance to taste it.

My sister after she sucked on a lemon!

FOODS THAT ARE **BITTER**

CABBAGE

BRUSSELS SPROUTS

SPINACH

LIMES

GRAPEFRUIT

There Are Chocolate Trees

TRUE   OR   FALSE   CIRCLE ONE

Yes. It's true. There really are chocolate trees. Chocolate is made from cocoa powder. And cocoa powder is made from the seeds of the cacao tree. I bet you think I didn't spell the name of this tree right. But I did and you pronounce it like this—*kuh-KAH-o*—while the name of the powder is pronounced KO-*ko*.

Cacao trees are hard to grow and never get very tall. They need to be close to the equator where it is very wet and warm. They usually grow in rain forests.

MAP OF WHERE CACAO TREES GROW

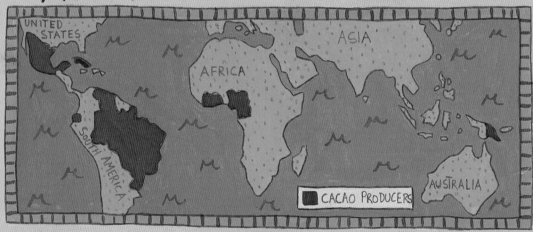

UNITED STATES · ASIA · AFRICA · SOUTH AMERICA · AUSTRALIA · ■ CACAO PRODUCERS

HOW TALL IS THE CACAO TREE?

UP TO 60 FEET TALL IN THE WILD

← MAN

ONLY 15 FEET TALL ON A FARM

← MAN

This is what a cacao tree looks like. It has hundreds of tiny flowers that grow right on the trunk, as well as on the branches. Only a few of the flowers will produce fruit. The fruit doesn't look like apples or oranges or any other fruit you know. It looks weird—like something from a science-fiction movie.

The scientific name of the cacao tree is *Theobroma cacao*. Theobroma means "food of the gods."

TURN THE PAGE AND TAKE A LOOK

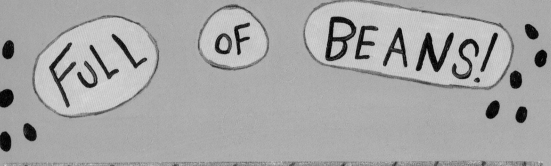

FULL OF BEANS!

HERSHEY CHOCOLATE CORPORATION
HERSHEY, PA.

The fruit from a cacao tree is called a pod and each one is the size of a football! The outside is very hard, like wood. You need a big knife to split one open. Inside is lots of white pulp and 30 to 40 beans, which kind of look like almonds. These beans are what make chocolate. Today, most of the cacao beans come from Africa.

I GROW ABOUT 40 PODS A YEAR.

CACAO PODS TURN

RED   ORANGE   YELLOW

WHEN THEY ARE RIPE.

Once they're scooped out of the pod, the beans are kept covered for about a week. During this time, changes start to take place inside the beans, and they turn dark brown.

Then the beans are dried out in the sun and sent to a factory. There, they get roasted. (It takes about an hour.) The thin shells are removed, and the beans are crushed into a thin paste called chocolate *liquor*. Don't worry! This kind of liquor doesn't have any alcohol in it.

Chocolate liquor is the main ingredient in chocolate. It takes about 400 beans to make a pound of chocolate.

WHO WERE THE FIRST CHOCOLATE LOVERS?

Canada

United States

Mexico

South America

Mexico

Guatemala

Deep in the jungles of Mexico and Guatemala are tombs that are more than a thousand years old. Kings and rich people are buried inside, along with their most valuable possessions, including cacao beans and special griddles for roasting them. Obviously, chocolate was something very special, something the people wanted to have with them even after they died. Who were these first chocoholics? They were the ancient Mayan people.

IF YOU WERE REALLY RICH YOU GOT TO HAVE A BIG PYRAMID FOR A TOMB.

LOTS OF STEPS

Sweet.

HONEY IN JUG

Jugs in some tombs still had traces of chocolate drink. This showed that the Mayans drank their chocolate unsweetened, with maybe a dash of honey.

Spicy.

BLACK PEPPER AND SPICY CHILI PEPPER IN JUG

Sometimes the chocolate drink had traces of spices like black pepper and spicy chili pepper. So the ancient Mayans must have liked their chocolate with a kick!

MEANS "THE HOUSE"

I like to eat chicken *mole* at Mexican restaurants. Mole is chocolate sauce, but it's not sweet.

You say it like this—*moh-lay*.

SOMETIMES MOLE CAN BE MADE WITH AS MANY AS 28 INGREDIENTS

CHOCOLATE MONEY

In the 1200s, the Aztec people, who also lived in Mexico, conquered the Mayans. Guess what! The Aztecs discovered that they liked chocolate, too.

A famous Aztec emperor was named Montezuma. He loved drinking chocolate so much that he let the Mayans pay their taxes in cacao beans. Soon, cacao beans were being used as money.

TURKEY EGG

3 BEANS

TURKEY HEN

100 BEANS

FEATHER CAPE

1,000 BEANS

Sometimes, people say, "Money doesn't grow on trees."
But for the Aztecs, it did. One book I read said that a turkey
egg cost three beans, a live turkey hen cost 100 beans, and
for 1,000 beans, you could buy a feather cape.

But people had to watch out that they were paid real cacao
beans. Forgers made fake beans out of clay.

THE CHOCOLATE BANK

16 CUPS TO GO.

Montezuma is said to have drunk more than 50 cups of chocolate a day. And while he had a fortune in gold, Montezuma also had a cacao bean bank.

I read that it held millions of beans. I guess the emperor wanted to make sure he never ran out of chocolate. Makes sense to me!

In the 1500s, Spanish explorers sailed across the Atlantic Ocean to the New World. They were looking for gold. And the Aztecs had plenty of that. Montezuma served the explorer Hernando Cortez chocolate in golden goblets. This was something he had never tasted before.

When he returned to Spain, not only did he bring Aztec gold, he also took some of Montezuma's cacao beans, and the recipe for the chocolate drink.

How Sweet It Is!

The Spanish ruler Prince Philip tasted the chocolate drink and decided to give it a new twist. He added something else that the explorers brought from the New World—cane sugar. Presto! Sweetened chocolate.

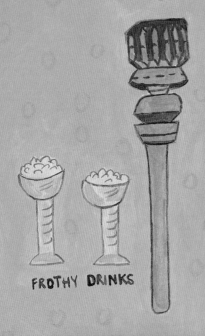

FROTHY DRINKS

THE SPANISH CREATED A TOOL, THE MOLINILLO (Moh-lin-YEE-oh) TO MAKE WHIPPING UP FROTHY DRINKS EASIER.

WHO SPILLED THE BEANS?

It took about a hundred years before other European countries discovered the joy of chocolate. One book said that pirates stole the recipe for chocolate from sailors on Spanish ships. In another book, I read that a Spanish princess took the recipe with her when she married a French King in 1615.

Whichever way the recipe spread, drinking chocolate became very popular for rich people all over Europe.

CHEAP CHOCOLATE

YEAH, CHOCOLATE FOR US!

By 1730, a machine was invented to grind cacao beans. Now, chocolate could be made much more cheaply. It wasn't just for rich people anymore.

In the United States in 1780, a chocolate mill started making and selling chocolate powder. It was called "BAKER'S Chocolate," and it is still sold today.

BAKER'S CHOCOLATE IS USED FOR BAKING DELICIOUS TREATS.

BROWNIES

CHOCOLATE CAKE

CHOCOLATE PUDDING

CHOCOLATE MILK

CHOCOLATE PIE

FUDGE

In 1847 a company in England decided that people might like to eat chocolate as well as drink it. Cocoa powder and sugar were combined with water and melted cocoa butter. Then the mixture was poured into molds and left to harden. Ta-da! The first chocolate bar.

COGOA POWDER + SUGAR + WATER + MELTED COGOA BUTTER = CHOCOLATE BAR

In just a few years, companies were making all kinds of chocolate candies . . . bonbons, chocolate creams, caramels, and "boiled sweets"—creamy flavored candies dipped in chocolate.

Back then, the only kind of chocolate was dark, or semisweet chocolate. In order to use less cocoa powder, some candy-makers added ground-up dried peas, then stirred in powdered bricks to make the chocolate darker! That's gross!

PEAS + BRICKS = YUCK!

A Swiss chocolate-maker wanted to make chocolate creamier, so he came up with the idea of adding milk. But regular milk—even cream—wasn't thick enough. All he got was chocolate-flavored milk. Finally, he discovered that condensed milk did the job. (Condensed milk has most of the water in it removed.) Once condensed milk was mixed into melted chocolate, the result was creamy *milk chocolate*!

Today, milk chocolate is the most popular chocolate in the United States—92 percent of all the chocolate sold. People in Europe still like dark, bittersweet chocolate better. (I'm not a big fan of bittersweet chocolate.)

CHOCOLATE TOWN, USA

Last summer, my family visited Hershey, Pennsylvania, home of Hershey's Chocolate. The world's biggest chocolate factory is there.

Milton Hershey was born in 1857 in Pennsylvania. By trying out different recipes, he came up with his famous milk chocolate. In 1903 he built a chocolate-making factory. He also built a town for his workers.

MY HERO

CANDY STORE

BET I COULD MAKE BETTER CHOCOLATE.

CANDY FOR SALE.

I'll JUST MAKE MY OWN CHOCOLATE.

 First, he had a candy store. But it failed. Then he sold candy. He didn't make money from that, either. Then he decided to make his own chocolate . . . good idea, Milton.

HERE IS MILTON HERSHEY WITH SOME SCHOOL CHILDREN.

I LIKE IT HERE.

ME TOO!

Milton Hershey wanted his workers to be happy. He had nice houses built for them—no two were exactly the same. He made sure the town included a park, schools, a zoo, a community center, and a grand hotel.

Anyone coming to the factory has no trouble finding it. You go down Cocoa Avenue until you reach East Chocolate Avenue. How great to have that for your address! The street lamps are also shaped like Hershey's Kisses. No wonder it's nicknamed "Chocolate Town."

ISN'T THIS A GREAT STREET LAMP?

BEAN TO BAR

I took a trolley and then I found out how chocolates are made.
I never knew machines could make so much candy so fast.

 First, milk is blended with sugar. It becomes like taffy.

2 Then chocolate liquor is added and the mixture is dried. The result is a crumbly chocolate powder.

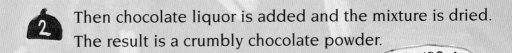

IT TAKES A LOT OF WORK TO MAKE CHOCOLATE.

3 Next, cocoa butter is added to create a chocolate paste. This paste passes through steel rollers to make it smoother. Then it is poured into huge vats, where granite rollers whip the paste until it turns into creamy milk chocolate. That can take three days.

BEAN TO BAR

Now, the chocolate is poured into molds, as many as 1,000 molds per minute, to create Hershey's milk chocolate bars. The molds are shaken to remove air bubbles from the chocolate and then passed through a chilling tunnel. Finally, the solid chocolate bars are wrapped and packed for shipping.

I don't like kisses very much, but I sure like Hershey's Kisses. Nobody really knows how Hershey's Kisses got their name, but some people think it might be because the chocolate makes a sound like a kiss when it comes out of the machine. Hershey's Kisses are the most popular packaged candy in the entire USA. Hershey has to make about 33 million Kisses a day just to keep up!

My sister last Halloween

JUNK FOOD or HEALTH FOOD

CIRCLE ONE

Chocolate is definitely *not* junk food. It has a small amount of protein and is high in carbohydrates, which help your body stay active and healthy.

That's why, in 1911, the explorers Roald Amundsen and Robert Falcon Scott both took chocolate with them on the race to reach the South Pole. And during World War II, U.S. and British soldiers carried chocolate bars in their packs. In fact, M&M's were first produced for soldiers as a treat that wouldn't melt in their pockets. Chocolate is also part of the U.S. astronauts' food supply.

Chocolate isn't health food, either. It does contain a small amount of caffeine. That's the chemical in coffee and tea that gives people a "pick-me-up" feeling. But you would have to eat more than a dozen chocolate bars to get as much caffeine as there is in one cup of coffee.

AT BREAKFAST THE OTHER DAY, I TRIED TO GET MY MOM TO DO THE CHOCOLATE EXPERIMENT, BUT SHE WOULDN'T GIVE UP HER COFFEE.

HEY, MOM, I'LL TRADE YOU ALL THESE CHOCOLATE BARS FOR YOUR ONE CUP OF COFFEE.

UM... NO, THANKS.

Chocolate candy has a lot of sugar and fat in it, so it's high in calories. Eating some is just fine, as long as you eat lots of other food that's good for you.

THINGS LIKE FRUITS AND VEGETABLES

CARROTS

BREAD

NOODLES

CHEESE

MEAT

EGGS

JUICE

TOMATOES

GRAPES

BANANAS

WHY DOES CHOCOLATE MELT IN YOUR MOUTH?

That's a question I always wondered about. After all, hamburgers don't melt in your mouth; neither does corn on the cob—two of my other favorites. So, I did an experiment and you can do it, too (if a grown-up says okay).

1. Put 20 semisweet chocolate chips into a Ziploc plastic sandwich bag. Squeeze out the air before you seal it shut.

2. Set the bag in a bowl in the sink. Add a half cup of cool tap water.

3. Place an indoor-outdoor thermometer in the water, wait five minutes, and check the water's temperature.

4. Have a grown-up add hot tap water to the cool water one tablespoon at a time, until you see the chips start to melt.

5. Check the water temperature again.

You'll see the chocolate first change from a solid to a liquid at about 84F. Normal temperature for a person is about 98F. So people are hot enough to melt chocolate! That's why it will melt in your mouth. Chocolate will also melt in your hand. (M&M's don't, because of the sugar coating.)

I'M SO HOT, I CAN MELT CHOCOLATE.

MY DAD MAKING A JOKE

CHEWY CHOCOLATE YUM-YUMS

I invented my own chocolate candy. It tastes pretty good, if I do say so myself. Ask a grown-up to help you make it.

Here's what you need:

USE A BIG BOWL

waxed paper
mixing bowl
wooden spoon
2 cups crunchy chow mein noodles
1 cup mini marshmallows
1 12-ounce package of chocolate chips

TRY NOT TO EAT ALL THE CHOCOLATE CHIPS OUT OF THE BAG BECAUSE YOU NEED THEM FOR THE YUM-YUMS.

Here's how to make it:

1. Pour the noodles and marshmallows into a mixing bowl.
2. With a grown-up's help, melt the chocolate chips in the microwave or in a pan on the stove.
3. Have the grown-up pour the melted chocolate into the bowl. Stir well.
4. Spoon the chocolate-coated noodles and marshmallows onto waxed paper. Wait until the mixture cools a bit.
5. Shape the spoonfuls into balls about the size of Ping-Pong balls.
6. Put the candy in the refrigerator.
7. EAT and ENJOY!

When I grow up, maybe I'll be a chocolatier. That's a fancy French word for someone who makes chocolate. You pronounce it like this—*shawk-latt-tee-yay*.

ME IN MY CHEF HAT!

OLDIES BUT GOODIES

I was surprised that some of the chocolate candy I like best has been around for a long time.

1900 The first Hershey's milk chocolate bar was sold.

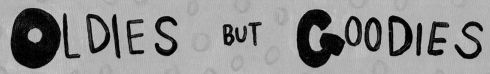

1907 Hershey's Kisses hit the market. During World War II, the company stopped making them, because the metal for the silver foil was needed for other uses.

1920 Baby Ruth candy bars were launched by the Curtiss Candy Company. Some people claim this candy bar was named after President Grover Cleveland's daughter; others say it's for the home-run king, Babe Ruth.

1926 Milk Duds first appeared in stores. They were supposed to be perfectly round, but since they weren't, these bite-sized candies were called "duds."

CHOCOLATE SURPRISES

I enjoyed finding out about chocolate for my report.
I even discovered some things that surprised me:

Americans don't eat the most chocolate. The Swiss do—
22 pounds per person a year. The average person in the U.S.
only eats about 10 pounds a year.

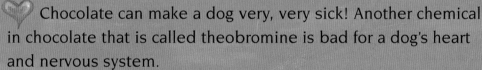

I HAVE NO IDEA HOW TO SAY IT!

Chocolate makes you feel good. It contains a chemical
called "**phenylethylamine**" (PEA) that makes a person feel
happy. Maybe that's why people often give their sweet-
hearts a box of chocolates.

DON'T GIVE ME CHOCOLATE.

GIVE THE DOG A BONE.

HAPPY

Chocolate can make a dog very, very sick! Another chemical
in chocolate that is called theobromine is bad for a dog's heart
and nervous system.

The biggest chocolate-buying holiday is not Valentine's
Day. It is Halloween, followed by Easter, the winter holidays
(Christmas, Hanukkah, and Kwanzaa), and then Valentine's
Day. Mother's Day didn't even make the list.

Gray blotches on chocolate do not mean the candy is
spoiled. It means the candy started to melt and then hardened
again. The discoloring, called a "bloom," spoils the look, but
not the taste.

CHOCOLATE BOOKS

I love chocolate so much that some of my favorite books are about chocolate:

Chocolate Fever by Robert Kimmel Smith

Henry Green loves chocolate, but after eating a lot of it, he breaks out in brown spots. He even smells just like chocolate. At the hospital, Henry finds out that he has the world's first case of Chocolate Fever.

The Chocolate Touch by Patrick Skene Catling

John Midas thinks he's been granted the best power ever when he discovers that everything his lips touch turns to chocolate. He thinks he can finally have all of the chocolate he could ever want. Then he kisses his mom and she turns into chocolate, too!

Charlie and the Chocolate Factory by Roald Dahl

Charlie Bucket becomes one of the five lucky kids who win a tour of Willy Wonka's Chocolate Factory. It's a mysterious, magical factory where some pretty amazing things happen. Then the tour winners get into trouble when some of the children eat too much and won't listen to what the adults tell them.

Superfudge by Judy Blume

This book actually isn't about chocolate. It's about a boy and his pesty younger brother, whose nickname is Fudge. But it's funny and I really like it.